THE DIFFERENCE BETWEEN

GRANT HIER

The Difference Between by Grant Hier

ISBN: 978-1-938349-86-7

eISBN: 978-1-938349-87-4

Layout and Book Design by Grant Hier and Mark Givens

pg. 1: from *Chemistry* (9th Edition) by Steven and Susan Zumdahl, Brooks/Cole, 2013

pg. 3: from *The Effects of Mental Practice on the Acquisition of a Perceptual-motor Skill* by Thomas E. Samuels, Washington State University Department of Psychology, 1969

pg. 9: from *Home Ground: Language for an American Landscape*, Trinity University Press, 2006

pg. 77: from *The Power of Myth*, by Joseph Campbell, Doubleday, 1988

pg. 81: "Arithmetic" by Carl Sandburg, from *New Section*, 1933

First Pelekinesis Printing 2018

For information:
Pelekinesis, 112 Harvard Ave #65, Claremont, CA 91711 USA

Library of Congress Cataloging-in-Publication Data

Names: Hier, Grant, 1956- author.
Title: The difference between / by Grant Hier.
Description: Claremont, CA : Pelekinesis, [2018]
Identifiers: LCCN 2018014763 (print) | LCCN 2018014826 (ebook) |
ISBN 9781938349874 (ePub) | ISBN 9781938349867 (pbk.)
Classification: LCC PS3608.I329 (ebook) | LCC PS3608.I329 A6 2018
(print) |
   DDC 811/.6--dc23
LC record available at https://lccn.loc.gov/2018014763

www.pelekinesis.com

THE
DIFFERENCE
BETWEEN

BY

GRANT HIER

Grant Hier 2019

THE DIFFERENCE BETWEEN

The Difference Between Thou and That

THE DIFFERENCE BETWEEN SCIENCE AND NATURE

THE DIFFERENCE BETWEEN NATURE AND OTHER

THE DIFFERENCE BETWEEN OTHER AND US

THE DIFFERENCE BETWEEN US AND TIME

THE DIFFERENCE BETWEEN DIFFERENTIATION
AND WORD PLAY

THE DIFFERENCE BETWEEN WORD PLAY
AND DIALECTICS

THE DIFFERENCE BETWEEN DIALECTICS AND SCIENCE

FOREWORD

At my imaginary dinner party of luminous philosophers and poets, I seat Grant Hier next to Gaston Bachelard. Had their time on earth in physical form overlapped past Hier's toddlerhood, and had I been able to arrange an actual party, a lively conversation would surely have ensued. As Bachelard said in *The Poetics of Space*, "To mount too high, or descend too low, is allowed in the case of poets who bring earth and sky together," and bringing earth and sky together is precisely what Hier does in *The Difference Between*. Out of difference, an almost indescribable unity emerges, and this is the territory of Hier's poetry.

This is a fabulous book and I am honored to say so.

These poems are not easily excerpted, because every line and every word is inevitable and necessary to the whole. Disclaimer given, here is a stanza from "The Difference Between the Thread of the Current and the Present":

> Like grief's erosion, how the stone exposed shows
> new colors as parts lift away. How as long
> as the core remains we hold onto order, even
> with gravity insisting on return,

This book is astonishing in its scope. In addition to the weighty matters it confronts, it is full of intelligent humor and word play as evidenced by one of my favorite poems, "The Difference Between Assonance and Camouflage." Hier pulls from mathematics, physics, music, the natural world in all of its manifestations, and from the mysteries of the human heart to create a poetry of wonder.

As I put down *The Difference Between*, these lines spoken by Thesues in *Midsummer Night's Dream* seem a perfect coda for the book:

> The poet's eye, in fine frenzy rolling,
> Doth glance from heaven to Earth, from Earth to heaven.
> And as imagination bodies forth
> The forms of things unknown, the poet's pen
> Turns them to shapes and gives to airy nothing
> A local habitation and a name.

I suspect Gaston Bachelard would agree.

—Donna Hilbert, author of *Gravity: New & Selected Poems*

To this vast similitude,
both the waves and the water.

The Difference Between Thou and That

Because there is no difference
between the wave and the water, the shape
one takes for the moment—for all
we know, it is not enough.

It is still, in the center; we know enough
not to take this moment as all,
yet it is—for between the shape
of wave and calm, the one. No difference

between the matter of each thing and its shape,
between the molecules and the force that holds it all
in place—because it matters not the difference
we perceive, only that we hold each other, is enough.

This is both the question and the answer,
the wave and the water—this is both.

THE DIFFERENCE BETWEEN SCIENCE AND NATURE

The Difference Between Entropy and Evaporation

"A process is said to be spontaneous if it occurs
without outside intervention."

—*Chemistry* (9th edition) by Steven and Susan
   Zumdahl, 2013

After the thunder, after the pouring,
after the sun and the warming,
the rain lifts itself back up
through its past.

The log collapses in the hearth,
the ash plume rising
in the place
of the old fire.

The bird in migration returns
through stilled eddies of ghost wing—
a mirrored image
of its younger self.

The pile of dirt dug from the garden
displaces the sky
in the same shape as the hole
in the earth beside.

Ancestors echo themselves
back alive through our gestures,
through scripted codes
unseen within us.

But first the kiss:
Spontaneous.

In the chilled air of morning, one bell

splashes awake, vibrates waves
up and down its shell
in pulses—

a blossom of tones
like colors,
like smoke,
like breath released

into another's mouth
in a whisper or moan—
a sharing of molecules, of sky
both inside and out.

Continuous change
brings irreversible paths
as heated prayers transform night,
but no bonds broken

here.
Here

as the sun
through the shade
casts the shadow
of the lamp

up the wall
as the day slides down,
our molecules warm
the cooling room

and you in your dressing
gown undressing—
a change of state,
a type of escape.

The Difference Between Practice and Play

"Judging from these data, mental practice can facilitate the acquisition of a perceptual-motor skill as readily as can physical practice."
—Thomas E. Samuels, Ph.D.

Imagine this:
The concert pianist plays
the table in front of him.
Eyes closed as he sways
and imagines the staves
as a stream, the notes
floating by on the current,
his hands chasing them
one finger-press at a time,
in time. The score plays
along in his brain—as if
the breakfast table were
a piano keyboard, as if
there were hammers
responding, striking
wires, sounding the stream
he sees in his head.
Hears in his head.
His brain lighting up
the same as when he is
in the hall and his Steinway
vibrates and pulses and booms,
and the air warms and shakes
the room alive, as the audience,
eyes shut, beams the same.
Neurons sparking internally,

identically—whether he's
playing or playing
like he's playing—ivory
or walnut at his fingertips,
struck strings ringing or
the dull thumps of finger-pads
reharvesting the wood.
The fire is lit within,
either way, just the same.

Now imagine
a crowd gathered in the concert hall,
listening as the orchestra vibrates
as one, and the air warms and shakes
the room, and all ears take in the struck
timpani's *ba-tum*—kettle drum sung
alive again within each skull chamber
there—here now—now the same.

Now imagine
yourself in the dark
in your kitchen. Tea kettle
singing the warble of morning,
rattle of lid, sizzle of metal
re-orchestrating spray—
your brain lighting up
with each sound played
in your head, both then
and now, the same.

Imagine:
our shared stories
of spark and line, river
and ritual, inner colors
to splash the night

alive in each of us
in the dark in bed,
in the room where
you are now—glorious.

The Difference Between the Love of Poetry and Sleepwalking

In somnambulism
no REM:

the dreaming
ends.

A twilight
realm.

The sleepwalker
talks

a language
of gibberish.

Yet from within
it may well be poetry—

or the tongue of angels
(which may also be poetry—

assuming angels exist).
Those awake see only

strangeness
in such blank gazes

and unexpected
shufflings,

as if trying to decipher
cuneiforms.

But the sleepwalker
is fluent in that tongue,

a logician in that realm
of nonsense phrases—

as the one in love
is mesmerized

with half-
glazed eyes.

What do they see?
They look the same.

As if some invisible
animal force compels them.

They walk a few feet
above the ground—

not in the clouds
but along the seam

between the world
of before

and the promise
of what could be.

Delta waves
slow the brain.

Neurons
in the busy

neocortex
go silent

to rest
at last.

Such are the shifts
that can break us

free as the quietest
places then awaken.

Deadened eyes
strangely open.

Pupils dilate
as walls fall away

to open
spaces—

an open
landscape.

Glassy stares
truss the niches

between new donnings
and what is shed there,

new worlds and what is
shared there.

Not the words
so much

as the places
those words take us.

The Difference Between The Thread of the Current and the Present

(after "Arrowhead" by Robert Wrigley)

"The *thread of the current*, the mathematical line
of the greatest rapidity...exceeds...the average
speed of the river...sometimes on the surface of
the river, sometimes a few feet below...Forming,
so to speak, a river in the middle of a river...
perceptibly higher."
—from *The earth and its inhabitants. The
    universal geography* by Élisée Reclus, 1876

"*fil du courant*: A Cajun French term meaning
'thread of the current'... The fil is often visible as
a glassy-smooth pathway through the otherwise
ripping water."
—from *Home Ground: Language for an American
    Landscape,* 2006

That the Earth attracts all things near it nearer,
compels us equally. It seems that way. That even
in the path of least resistance things will delay
and resist, like pooling wells in lightning and water.

Even within the tension bides a quiet
resolution, eventual release.
That entropy seems a law within every
realm imagined or observed, and still,

we see a tendency in each gesture, in every
being, to shine order, as to remind.
This too: That opposites, even
the whole of us, can be reflected in one

being, in one thing. The river stone,
for instance—still and smooth beneath the stream,
glistening in the sun just now, and how
it matches your laugh, the sky reflected in it

somehow, both the weight and the freedom, the
clear path shining in the midst of movement. As
the current bulges and time thickens in my chest,
your eyes as clear as the depths here, but deeper.

Like grief's erosion, how the stone exposed shows
new colors as parts lift away. How as long
as the core remains we hold onto order, even
with gravity insisting on return,

the leveling at the mouth. We resist, but a long
run of continuous change is the thread followed
down this temporary present, the gift
that keeps things new. Young rivers run the fastest,

past steeper slopes, the course straighter for such
speed, the river becoming part of the ground
it penetrates, and the exchange spontaneous
as what has been displaced now becomes river

in a weaving of elements, a song of valence,
the change of landscape gradual, the trees
creaking as they sway, the wind sliced
by Aeolian harps of branches and needles, now part

of the chorus recalling the sound of the sea far
downstream, awaiting past the slower shallows,
the winding down of current time as the old
river widens and quiets and meanders to its end.

Just as this day winds down and long shadows
soften, the cold progressing in increments
until we finally notice through our shivering,
and I take off my coat and you slide it on, smiling,

dressing in the warmth of this gift, the heat transferred,
and new faces as we step from stone to stone
to the other side, slower now, in even steps,
in tandem. And along with my outstretched hand

I can offer you this: That even as the stones
become undone beneath us, even now
as the darkness progresses, I promise I will hold
the light that you emit now, now without

even realizing it, even
when this crossing is done. Know that I
have found it behind you, too, in the flashing water,
the bits of sun carried back to me, even

as parts of us are leaving. Even as I write,
"whichever of us leaves first," know this:
That some things will reach across
to balance—the river's lesson returned in light.

THE DIFFERENCE BETWEEN
NATURE AND OTHER

The Difference Between Never Uncovered and Discovered

Under becomes over
when digging a hole.

Over isn't over
until forgotten.

You'll wonder
what has become

of the lover
you once

thought of
in terms of

forever.
You'll never

know
the rest

until you lift
the covers.

The Difference Between Sacrifice and Afterlife

Once the tree has fallen
it becomes something else.
Once it pointed to another
realm that was clear and bright
half of the time, full of stars
the other. Once fallen, it might
point to the other side of the river
and/or might be the bridge to it.
It might be just as important
in its horizontal state as it was
in its upright existence. Or, it
might hold some other importance.
In it we might find some options
we had not thought of for
a purpose beyond what we
thought was the purpose.

Once the tree has fallen
we might learn how to look
at purpose in a whole new way.
Once fallen, decay might be
a bridge to new life beyond
which follows ours, rising
perpendicular from where we fell
and into the same sky we once
occupied before it. A new thing
built from/upon those parts we
offered ourselves/of ourselves.
All we offered and what was
melded from it might point
to some new shore then. Or it
might be the bridge to it. And/or
something else more important.

The Difference Between Ecology and Environment

Without trying
  the Earth spins.
    It was set in motion
      somehow. Evolves
        as it revolves.

All in,
  is how we live
    (or should),
      holding nothing back
        as we play out our days.

At this stage
  we do more than react.
    We act, and act (or should)
      to control how we move though
        this world, and how we leave it.

The Difference Between Conveyance
and Passing Through

For the yellow banded bee inside the blossom,
the light is indirect, diffused, encompassing.
The jointed antennae sense whatever they can
from the air. Thick fuzz of hair on the thorax
regulates temperature, picks up pollen from
the stamen, carries it on to the tip of the pistil
of the next open flower—transference the goal.

Angle of sun determines the route, and
shadows show what's been blocked
(as the psychologist said). Presence proven
by opacity: how much spectrum we absorb or
reflect, how much love we can carry with us
(even as some waves pass right through us).
We seek the wherewithal to hold—what then?

Each other? Yes. But for how long?
Trust and sparks. The memory of scent
and essence. But it's all shifting light
and the sticky dark. Everything we see
we claim to know, but what if all the light
that reaches us is just a form of dusk:
neither fully upon us or absent,

and sliding either toward or away?
All things muted. Our sensors dull.
Always a lack of full-spectrum knowledge
in this world. In this world,
always some heavy coat carried,
always something turned away.
Always a degree of uncertainty
(as the scientist said).

All the suns can do
is radiate in all directions.
Up to us, then, to take in
what we can, while we can.
Simple.
Yet we find we're short on time.
Whatever light we have

and what it falls upon
is how we gauge our days—
might be how we, in turn,
are measured back. How we react.
How we reciprocate, however awkwardly.
Our shadows show our form,
if not our grace.

The Difference Between the Song Within the Bird and What is Heard

Whatever the thrush was thinking before
she opened her throat to sing. What was felt
in her drumming breast during flight.
The echoes that pulsed
through her hollow bones
at rest. (These are what
I seek to know.)

The long stare and the clever words before
we open up. Notes shared to bring wellness
and strength for the coming test of
night. Who knows what else
might follow us home.
The rest we seek. (What
we cease to know.)

The Difference Between Futility and Down

The pet bird's beak clips the newspaper page
into meticulously even strips, long and thin,
edges echoing the shape of the beak's curve.
She pecks and picks up each one once she finishes,
twists her head and slips them deep into her
back mantle of feathers, the edited news
of yesterday swaying behind her as she turns
back to the front page, returning to the place
she left off, the one edge already finished.
With each replacement feather she creates,
her beak swipes across her preen gland
at the base of her tail, and she nibbles
and strops the new paper pride she has
placed there between her wings. Her wings—
they were clipped before she ever tried to fly,
blood-feathers dripping, crippling her.
Now, daily frustrated feather plucking
and fake plugs carefully placed there to
replace the bare spots. The farmed goose
in China was scalded so its skin would soften,
its feathers then harvested by a loud machine
that followed its contours as the wind might
have during flight. The man who purchased
bird and cage and bedding, who read the news
that will be shaped into tomorrow's feathers,
he now covers the cage with a black cloth
and turns off the light. And now he moves
his thin lips methodically around the shape
of a prayer asking for cover for all once laid
bare. He imagines it soaring up into the night.
Then his head on cotton pillowslip sinks down
into the down and he dreams of flight.

The Difference Between One and Reunion

Repeating the sunrise, the chirping bird
fills itself with the world, sings
it back in a puff, bob, and whistle—
cacophony to the bee in the flower
nuzzling, the thirst for more, deeper
still. The head twists in a blur
to clear the senses. A new realm.
The first dawn must have been like this.

You and I were there, as star-
ash, scattered in atoms not
yet gathered into the us we are—
just a lumbering shrug of bonding
here and there, perhaps a shudder
of recognition of what was to come:
the hum of promise the oak remembers
from the tumbling cupule fall. The thump.

And we wait between beats. Asleep
as the seasons repeat like a drum. Dreaming
the actor into being, the play resumes—
The rearrangement of ancient stories
into new ones, one sunrise
at a time, lines and acts repeated,
the lovers and the future assembled thus
in a shimmer like a placenta spilled,

or a surfacing fish. The wish for wholeness
rises and shines as we lie in the dark.
The thing we forget it this:
the song of sun in the bird,

the same arc and angle, the familiar
air. The oncoming light echoed
in a blur of stars between poles.
The hum in the wires. The letter from home.

THE DIFFERENCE BETWEEN
OTHER AND US

The Difference Between Rattle and Settling

If strung all together, consider the days we lose
pausing, flat gazed, in stasis. Imagine all of
the gaps between action linked like empty freight
cars, a preponderance of moments spent pondering
things no longer relevant—like the tea cup
on a glass shelf, empty but for a film of dust,
locked in a curio cabinet in the far back
of an antique store, perhaps a rattle
against the saucer when the train rolls by
on Sunday, shaking the stillness, a slow swirl
of motes stirred to motion, then the settling.

And on that train, a woman who is rushing away,
yet still in that world, lost in a thought of one day
at the ocean when she was twenty. How she
shuddered when he first kissed her there, as when
the liquor he offered burned a ribbon of warm
down her core, her heart a-flutter like an elixir
to the worry of being alone. Her fingers had
pressed white moons into his reddened back
and neck, but they faded like the stars diluted
into dawn, and slowly he would pale, then vanish
altogether. For one full summer she drank him in,

wore his clothes, tangled her limbs in his sheets,
adored the landscape of his mystery. She can no
longer recall his face. Pieces, yes: the close to
perfect lips she traced with hers. She had
thought love eternal, but all is now reduced
to a just a replay of one day, over and over,
like the looped background in a cartoon
from childhood. The fast train filled with slow
contemplation on what we've accepted without

pause, blurred scenes of what we'll never know
rushing past us, a still life. Yes. Still,

there is that stranger who saw you from
the crossing, to which you were a shadow
in a window that passed with a clatter, and that
was that. This is how life clears the tracks. We shift
in our seat and make do with comforters, remnants
stitched like half prayers half uttered. Resolution
and clarity gained by sinking impurities. A loose
floorboard that lifts a creak, a groan to stir the sound
of the living into someone's dream. The rest
that comes after all has been lost. The last cough
deep in the chest that rocks the bones before sleep.

The Difference Between Salt Water and Blood

Rather than drift,
better to swim, but
best to lean oneself fully
against the foghorn wind
in a coat, stitched by the hand
of a lover, who waves,
from that hand,
from a high dark window,
a scarf the soft color
of her throat at dusk,
tight and deep violet within,
that lining that warms you
even now, that you can not see,
a bright flag trailing her colors,
a soft tongue alive in the night
and singing in a gust of wind,
offered so that you might know,
so at last you might understand.

The Difference Between the Architect and Arcadia

Call it desolation: the suited man in 1964 standing at the edge of a new patch of sunlight, shivering. A monochromatic study: his gray unpainted pencils erect in a wire rack at work, 24 stories up, and far below his lighter slate perpendicular to a sea of deep grey concrete. He, the last to know amidst a downpour of first light warming the sidewalk after a night of drizzling rain. A letter, unread lead on grey paper, is folded sharply in his breast pocket. In it, clearly defined, are all of the reasons why she left, never articulated by her yet revealed in his sad asking, in lines meant to illustrate and convince— that her gardens of unordered stepping stones would be better if reconfigured into his Classical plans for the days ahead. And in his head all of the reasons why she should stay. An unwitting dirge in a minor key composed too late, clearly ordered like his architectural drawings stacked in drawers, or the staves of his beloved Schubert which he studies as he listens with his single malt late into the night. The formality, hierarchy, clean divisions between parts, sharp contrasts, and such simplicity. How could she not prefer this? But his cold lines, indented to sway, are what drives her away. (The irony of such a life as his unfolding into Romantic clichés—the neglected genius who dies in obscurity, alone, his best work unfinished.)

Call it action, he had told her: his decision to control things. Object lines kept thick for exterior walls. Dimension lines show the width and size. Hidden lines indicate what's found beneath. Center lines show rich symmetry. Thinner lines extend from object to dimension. Cutting-plane lines denote areas to be sectioned. Border lines darkest to enclose it all in, and all could be ordered like this, she and him, a clear future. No, order as verb—not that she would be ordered. He wasn't telling her what to do. Like the difference between "crepitate" and "crepitant," for instance, between making a crackling sound and having one. "One crepitates on crepitant leaves," his voice droning on, his hand chopping clouds of breath before his face, but she listened only to the crunch of her step, the scrape of a leaf's edge skidded ahead by her staggering gait.

Call it desperation. She was already gone. She never showed her inner tension—beyond the metaphorical memo of regrets pinned to her hair shirt, hidden under the periwinkle sweater she always wore on days like this, buttoned once, as if expecting inclement weather: not without climate, but showing no clemency or mercy, she had wanted to correct him—because he had written "inclimate" on her birthday card—but what would be the point? Ironic for the man who insisted on the fine print, precise symmetrical tips on drafting pencils, who would roll the shaft as he drew each line, careful with his T-Squares, triangles, arrows, but not with the weight his gestures carried. He always corrected her, the one he imagined a cornerstone, unaware of her own worth as load-bearer for him, her rising tower as a teacher, reaching for new heights for the both of them. He had thought he could undress her always dressing for defeat, he as her Pygmalion applying veneers of sophistication even with the glass of this Metropolis reflecting other towers, even with her need to run ahead and stand on tip-toes out in the forests north of this city, her lips mimicking the shape of knotholes, her arms stretching up toward a different blue than his old diazos and houseplans. A fresh Crayola in an unopened box, the tip a miniature flat plateau—never a point, really, but nothing holds it shape for long, so what if shrubs are cropped at the start, like reasons never explained, open spaces never filled in? The raw background tooth of the page suffices. Colors never pulled out have their own story—burnt siennas of earth she'd never seen plowed beneath her ancestor's land, indian red chestnut mare of her great-great-grandmother, brick red of old blood, goldenrod dawns, aquamarine nights, sky blue windows reflecting sky behind her and all she missed, the crayons that never once trailed lines to contain or filled in shapes or traced horizons for a bare-kneed girl in forest green slumber, dreaming of the flesh of fruit stacked in markets in a new bustling land, the raw umber hunger, the pale peach of nail moons in two clutching hands.

The Difference Between Falling In and Falling Out

So much so she had to laugh—
splash of warm bath over the edge
soaks the news of the day on the floor.

What she had thought she had wanted, unread—
she was not prepared for that.

The Difference Between Flammable and Incendiary

Everything she's projecting is in some way
a story of her helplessness and a longing
for the past to be replaced with this now.

And so, there was one arched eyebrow,
one signal half-smiled, and just enough
of a head tip to count as a nod. Yes.

Enough to warm a flutter and spark
a tip of the head in return.
Enough to burn a thought

that this dance was just for him,
the message private despite the room
and it was, yes, more than enough.

THE DIFFERENCE BETWEEN
US AND TIME

The Difference Between Restraint and Gravity
(After "Juggler" by Richard Wilbur)

These days will flatten more and more, and we will forget the domed ceilings our laughter once reached. The fall renounces summer heat, cuts left across oncoming traffic to rise with the solstice winds, the cold increasing with each block. Years before, at the equinox, she had dragged a sack to the edge of the green, prepared to set fire to whatever edges might be dry enough to burn. Now, she drops her gaze as she walks, her thoughts intent on how four best friends moved away in the span of just three seasons. Each step kicks a spray of sand ahead, soft whistles of friction punctuating each stride. She does not notice. Her gaze is inward, narrow and deep.

The ball of sun will widen as it drops into the sea, each day father south by a few degrees. Hardly noticeable unless one is set on marking such things (as she once was). The retrograde and clocks reset, then comes the forgetting, hand to head. The fields freeze, thaw. Ruts fill with black muck before still water can bounce heavy clouds back up off the ground. Silly of us, then, collecting small stones, accumulating phrases we decided not to share. Too much, too soon. Instead, we stared across ridges of beach that echoed the moving crests beyond, shared silent seams of rock, smooth surfaces that deepened when wet, revealing the impossible colors of glossy irises in magazine ads, pigmented cells beneath stroma, nebulae and planet pastels captured by

Hubble blinks. We juggled these things with our eyes not fixing on any one of them, each full moon surprising in its size and color rising through the trees. Each sun (but one) so far off we barely felt the heat. We dropped our shoes to rub the other's feet.

A future is easier made of chance, or imagined, than the past rearranged. We can't go back to utter what might have saved us, or re-jostle things once said to shift the stress or intent, and so– You cry out when no one can hear you, read "On the Beach at Night Alone," wonder why the pull of old orbits still keeps you off balance, if you are fated to this life of constant interruptions, always one or two things too many to hold, forever shuffling, nearly dropping, wondering if the choice to not pick up your feet or cross one block sooner matters to any degree, or if staying until the nocturne resolved into silence would have been a better choice. Instead, you imagine the stories implied by zigzag prints on wet sand. At the fruit stand, a paper sack of apples, each carefully selected by a reaching hand, now abandoned on the stack of bruised pears. Party balloons released and fading into azure until they are lost completely, the upturned stares dissolving below. Slow rain darkening the cement walk before us, one dark splotch at a time until it fills us completely and we burst into embrace.

If we are more tired now, if the books slip from our grip or our stories start to drop through the dark again beyond us, let them. Let us not clasp the other's open palms just to let go this time. Instead, let us both bring our own hands together—not to batter them in applause, or grasp out wildly at the air behind what cannot be saved, those things that sound and sail beyond the both of us. Let us celebrate the changing light and things that can manage to rise at all, however briefly, to whatever degree, and not rue the fall—for once, be one who has offered the world less weight.

The Difference Between Healing and Change

To the ocean comes a parent
wishing her child to taste the sea.
New remoteness in
the eyes of her since
the desert freeze. Hot
days lost in
that passing.

Comes a mother to the shore, sent
to sing her daughter's name. She's
now gone from view. Thin
cries in the wind, dance
of kites, the gulls not
joining in
but laughing.

The Difference Between Elevation and Joy

And the ocean was lifted slightly with
our presence, your entrance into its froth
buoyed both, what we displaced in its vastness.
With your slow walk into the breakers, stiff-
legged strides, arms held away from your sides
to stay dry (for the moment), you raising
your frame up on tiptoes, bouncing with each
wave you met (or that met you), and your wide
laughter drowned by the wind and boom of surf,
each loss a skipped stone. The sea level rose
with our union nightly. All the displaced
past, the world itself, seemed to elevate
with us, and we were one with each other
then, with everything (or so it seemed). In
those evenings that came before, we reclined,
wordless, to watch the tides and moon rise,
sliding a bright smudge opening through clouds,
as we wanted to, knowing the sea would
bring it back to us, shining from below.

The Difference Between Setting and Fixing

We begin to slow
as the day drifts
to soften. As the sun
nears the horizon,
colors thicken
in the distance.

All things redder
as blue light scatters,
our star a ruby
lowered to
its mounting,
the sea a tabletop,

our world
a theater awaiting
the dimming
of the lights.
All things slowing
with the coldness

until we turn and stop
and fix our gaze on
the widening disc
as it touches down.
It seems to rest
a beat and then—

drops faster somehow
in its disappearing,
our breathing
quickening with it,

as if some music
had started up,

as if the sky had
thinned. The cold
descends. The ball
of sun sinks with it
until just the edge—
just—

and we hold
our breath,
and then each other,
our arms blankets
offered to protect
against the coming night.

Then the Earth,
and we along with it,
release—resume
our slow turning
away—our earlier
colors draining to gray.

The Difference Between Rest and Remainder

Onto my feet first, I sample
the leftovers that prove better colder.
I make French press coffee and bring
it back—set one down by the clock,
one on the arm of the chair.
Let it sit as I sit. Let it release
its heat as it moves toward
the temperature of the room.
As I move my thoughts to
how things settle and layer,
the derivatives of our equality.

Given the simple lessons
of morning's walk of warmth
across the house, I let the light move
to me, gauge in silence our sensitivity
to change, let the sun (sifted through
the hedges and the window sash) slide
onto my feet first, then up my legs,
my chest, my neck—until you
finally shift as it reaches your neck
too, at the edge of the bed, and you
open your eyes and grin, squinting.

What we take away will be different.
I seek optimization. A solved equation
as the coffee cools and the space between
us warms. When I look to you again,
your gaze has shifted to a spot on the floor
between us, the balance point outside of
both of us—that place beyond flesh

and friendship where we sense the weight
of excess, as sheets are peeled away,
as we leap feet-first into the day,
the differentials of our want.

THE DIFFERENCE BETWEEN TIME AND PSYCHOLOGY

The Difference Between This Time and Forevermore

Remind, remind: The very end of time—isn't
that meaningless in this tick of the now?
The past tattoo of heartbeats makes us sick
just thinking about it. So don't. Listen to me.
Do not do it.

For looking up into the night, I cannot throw
my arms out wide enough, as far as I desire.
Not half as wide as my wonder. Not nearly
as long as I wanted, that last glance.
One day it will be, I know, I know.

Once the drunken ace of heartache ruled my
days. Confused awakenings: Dusk or dawn?
Dew or rheum? Then you, and the laughter
folded us over. Now, I can't get enough
this time. This time, be kind. Be kind,

now, and always, as I offer these poor
imitations of glory, these songs to your
fierce beauty, a timeless story.

The Difference Between Footprints and Hope

Future filled, we are,
the ballast of the past ever slowing:
to exist within a birth-blue seam—
sole of a foot unable to see
the ground upon which it stands.

Each day our face changes,
slow unfolding toward decay—
animal dander, dust mites, mold,
sloughed skin, insect debris, cells shed—and
strangers are shocked at how we've changed.

Step to go, the Now moves with us.
The Past but thread-worn impressions
and the frozen faces of clocks.
The Future, that last thing
to rise out of the box.

The Difference Between Experience and Appearances

A gradual shift is
almost like boredom.
Barely noticed. A shrug
as if, so what? The status quo.
No quid pro quo in temperature
or temperament exchanges.
Nothing rearranged.

A sudden change is
its own reward, though.
The world flashes newness
and snaps the head back so you
notice even more. That first bite
and burn of a Thai Dragon
Pepper, say, like being
bumped awake.

Capsaicin
jolts the neurons,
lies that you're on fire.
A second wave slams all senses
then, tingles the top of your scalp
and gets you twitching. Then endorphins
flood in and opiate receptors warm as dopamine
joins the party, your pleasure centers weave
feathers through the heat.

Contradictions fly
through the body,
swarming like starlings
darting in fluid formations—
those mesmerizing murmurations

with breakneck turns every few
breaths. A beautiful chaos.
And you are shaken.

It doesn't
look all
that
crazy
or arousing
from the outside—
oh but from the inside,

after you've finally decided
to do it and charge full-tilt into a
pain you know will crash your senses—
like when you thrash directly into that ice-
cold ocean on a day when the clouds have
blended the sky and horizon line to one,
with no sun there to warm or reassure—
that sudden diving in and your entire

being is reminded of its oneness in
an all-at-onceness, as everything
within is reset to freezing.

From that wild edge
where the winter
breakers arrive
in booming
froths of
white,

then—
Ah! The
jarring shift
in point of view

when all the mundane
and unremarkable
appearances get
reimagined.

From the
inside, the view
is nothing like from
the shore—the water eye-level
now, the heaving swells lifting your
shaking core until the scene is transformed.
And that transforms you then. And you awaken.

The Difference Between Resistance and Release

> "Loveliest of what I leave behind is the sunlight,
> and loveliest after that the shining stars, and the
> moon's face, but also cucumbers that are ripe,
> and pears, and apples."
> —Praxílla of Sícyon, c. 450

Yes, apples.
And pears certainly.
But cucumbers?
Too much like the rind
of watermelon in both taste and texture.
Blindfolded, you couldn't tell them apart.
Just as, some day, you might confuse
the double-click budge of a hinge
on a bedroom door as it's inched open
with the throaty *caw-ca-kick* of a screw
being driven its last centimeter of spiral
into the hard dry grain of maple.

Those same clicks
(released slowly, one at a time, staggered
sparse across decades as the metal spins
a slow pirouette in easing itself back out)
echo what we have found in the years
of settling spent between: clicking joints
survive in the rot surrounding,
despite all wishes of the flesh—
and I will ache with that last breath
for the smells and the tastes
of this world to travel with me,
even if they reek of rotting rind.

The Difference Between Knowing and Myopia

200,000 years ago
the one who cries before she laughs
lies on her back in the great desert basin
and measures with her outstretched hands
the size of the Milky Way.

2,100 years ago
the son and daughter ask the father
the exact weight of the chariot he told them
Helios drives anew each day in moving the sun
across the heavens.

The child just learning to count to 10
scoops the surf with a blue plastic shovel,
carefully ladles each into his pail,
and sings out a number
for each bucket dumped
as he measures out the ocean.

The pragmatic scientist
who insists on evidence,
studies hypotheses,
steadies her old dog by laying on hands
and calls upon all forces she can imagine,
and even some she can't.

The meditating monk is told to conjure
the face that he possessed
on the day before his parents met,
and suddenly realizes
he is an eyeball
trying to look at itself.

For the flea that lives for 1/100th of a second,
born on the tail of a 14-year-old dog
(ratio of human life to the universe),
how much of the dog can it comprehend,
much less what that dog was like as a pup,
much less the full tale of that dog's full life?

The lubberly ape of the future,
when he finds three playing cards
left at an ancient campsite,
how much of the missing deck
will he be able to construct

from just a 4 of clubs, 7 of hearts,
and queen of diamonds,
much less understand
the rules of Bridge, or the best way
to bid such an odd hand dealt?

THE DIFFERENCE BETWEEN PSYCHOLOGY AND POLITICS

The Difference Between Punctual and Punctuation

The ticket to fly is our rented nimbleness,
the single day's journey to other beds. But first,
the commitment to travel, to change places,
to break our punctuated equilibrium of day-
to-day stasis. What prompts such new lines?
For some, a new job. Others, a new romance.
Or the closure of the old one done in person
out of respect—to clarify meaning and intent,
and to make certain once and for all before
the final gaze and embrace. But first, the lack
of grace. And for the those delayed by doubts
or missed alarms or freeway lock-ups, the stiff-
legged dashes to the gates, the rolling carry-
ons careening on one wheel at the bumps
en route that twist the wrist, the wheels re-
leveling and loudening in their *click-ka-
clack* tattoo across the airport floor until
the rumpled runner arrives at the gates
at last, out of breath, and braces for the clock's
display of the time. And across the terminal,
those who opted for discounted fares sleep
across the seats, purses and backpacks
for pillows, arms draped over suitcases
beside, or tied to twine that's laced through
belt loops, a tentative security at best. No less
risky than riding with a few hundred strangers
who cough and sniffle in the recycled cabin
air the whole flight. However long, the layovers
are but a comma, a brief pause in the journey,
not the terminus, and soon forgotten. Not seen
by the travelers: those pensive ones in the towers,

looking out, looking out after them. Not seen
are the cumulative costs: the lost sleep,
the fossil fuel waste, trade-offs made with
those left behind, virus free-loaders, non-
native agricultural question marks being
carried in the cargo holds. Also not seen:
the elegance of the science that allows for
such lifting, the distances closed and the time
saved over the slower roads and tracks below.
But not forgotten: the open-armed runnings
of home-coming embraces, the stone-faced
child left behind and the card of blue scribbles
that reveal her spiraling confusion over such
hectic leavings, the green displays that record
the presence and progress of planes delayed
and planes arriving on-the-dot, the elegant arcs
traced across the globe at all hours—swooping
like threads in a tapestry or the blue, purple,
scarlet and gold of a high-priest's Ephod—
maps of flight paths like thousands of closed
parentheses to the concaves of the Earth below,
curved marks to enclose all of the asides,
the additions, the phrases of relationships
to be whispered with the intention of less stress.

The Difference Between Holes and Salvation

There's a white trailer parked
once a month across the street
in front of the elementary school—
unhitched and leveled with a jack
at one end, the side door open
to the gutter. On the street-side,
a panel of corrugated steel and the words
"Burden Free—Christian Education"
in yellow paint that flakes like
mustard seeds onto the black asphalt.

This morning a boy and girl
walked past the "Chapel On Wheels"
the boy asking: "What can you add
to a barrel to make it lighter?"
"Holes!" she shouted, slapping
the brown cross nailed above
the license plate, and both walked on.

I've seen adults genuflect to avoid
the low threshold as they stepped inside,
but I've never seen them leave. I've seen
children bound up the steps, only to emerge
stooped, their back-packs full—or leaning,
their arms cradling gold-leaf books with
something changed inside; some light
that has made their flesh heavier.

The Difference Between Faith and Floating

The scramble and panic at tip, flood, and flurry
as rats dart up ropes of a tilting mast,
as the old home of shadows and crumbs
becomes a watery womb. The way nature
reveals what was hidden by and by:
as the one system fails, the weakness
unseen in the seams, in the folding over
of such blemishes, rises. The hook is set.
The prayer sticks in the neck. She seeks
the daylight to cling to at last as the ballast
of hope replenished stops the rocking hull.
He watches her as she sleeps. The blankets
cool. Newborn lungs hung with salt water
are coughed clean. This new realm.
Still, shiny sinkers glint in bottom mud.
Pristine life jackets, save for one small
hole to open the sky. So much to fail.
Bladder gas expands as the rockfish is reeled
up, maw swell forcing the stomach inverted
past grey wire lips; the drowning diver
coughs his last gasp and sinks
like a lead messenger weight thrown
down the wire to slam the chamber shut
and trap a sample from darkness. This life.
Swallowed words. Discarded clothes
on the bedpost like lures,
the buoyancy of obscurity.

The Difference Between Reflection and Distraction

Doubt breaks the surface
that holds (held) the wholeness:
still-water mirroring a near-full moon.
It shatters the focus, scatters both surface
facsimile and the moon (mind). But worse,
concentration splits to skewness in waves
and one questions one's own competence
then: rippled dips (drips) and dark craters
mix with bits of crescent glints, cohesive
forces scatter to staccatoed thoughts—
shouts into a fan blades' whirring
that chops (chips) both curse
and confidence.

THE DIFFERENCE BETWEEN
POLITICS AND NARRATIVE

The Difference Between Comfort and Happiness
(these truths we hold)

You complain about the heat,
mop the back of your neck
and shake your head
as if to show
your disdain for the noon,
as if trying to jostle
the hypothalamus loose,
as if the knot at your throat
could slip with mere denial.

You could travel to cooler climates
but those homes have odd angled walls
that hold unfamiliar sleep. And this heat.

So then, either change it or be changed by it.
Or this: Stay, but change clothes.
The sweat-soaked shirt thrown into a creek
that you never noticed before,
the same sun alive on your back,
but now weightless and welcome.
Stand up to gain a new perspective
on the same place you thought you knew,
the horizon wider now, and you see:

That frozen ideal sheets off icy eaves;
your comfort and cause is embedded deep.
This is it. She is it. No others.

The field is filled with faces, like stars,
reaching limbs, and each branch bears
fulfillment apples, both tart and sweet,

but perfect for pies, cooling on sills, both,
both of you there, side by side,
and you know, yes, and you smile,
resting beside the water,
envious of no birds or beasts
in other idylls, other groves.

The Difference Between Repair and Reconstruction

   (after 9/11)

As I sleep, this house creaks
under the weight of wood on wood,
the crankiness of masonry tile as it grinds
against itself on the roof, like a pumice stone
dragged along the edge of a tooth,
the weakness of bones remembered
in such sounds. I should thank this day
for opening these wounds, for reminding
me of what is needed to either start over
or repair: the longing for wholeness
that urges soft tissue to speak its promise
to the torn skin beside, to whisper
that it could find a way to bind again,
not as new, but stronger for finding
again the pulse through the pain,
the cry, the first strains of song.

Headlong, Unforgiving

The hollow crack of the stag's horn
echoes blue down the mountain,
carried by the aching wind

downhill. The conflict unseen,
now discerned. Head to head
it must have been.

Painful and hard
as the issues
that separate

in icy air.
Full force.
Headlong.

Unforgiving.
That way, the break
was inevitable.

And a lone stag
finally bolts
out into the clearing,

dazed—
the cracked horn
sagging,

splintered,
tearing
at the quick.

And it is only
the weight of what is broken
that finally turns the head.

The Difference Between What Falls and What We Fail To See

The medicine of lines
redrawn in retrospect
heals and harms the rest of
what we meant to say. The
rest of what we meant to
say is found too late. It
cannot change the moment,
can not find the difference
now between the snow and
what then fell inside and
somehow landed with it.
Somehow ended with it.
History retold.
Worse: collateral
damage as we close,
thinking we're alone.

The Difference Between Beliefs and Actions

Some can't talk about it.
Some won't talk about it.
Some can't stop talking about it.

Some say that beyond their own lives
and beyond the universe
there is nothing.

Some say there's everything
that can ever be imagined, and then some,
and that it just goes on and on without end.

Some say they are absolutely sure
they know the truth. Some say there's no way
of knowing. Some say nothing.

Some say time is limited and an end
will surely come. Some say time is infinite,
like space, and neither one ends.

Some say time is an illusion,
and some say everything
is happening all at once.

Some say one spirit
once manifest as one of us
to take on everyone's mistakes

and pay for it all in one go.
Some say thirty-six hidden saints are always
alive at any one time and on their shoulders

the virtues of the entire world rests—
that though they pass unnoticed among us,
our song always soars in their chests.

Some say the weight
and the lightness of the universe
is shared by each of us equally.

Some say there is no structure
or story except what we invent, and that
is both our burden and our freedom.

Some say all is divine.
Some say nothing is sacred.
Some say nothing.

Some say when this life ends
there is paradise, but only for some.
Some say paradise is right here.

Some say nothing exists beyond this one life.
Some say we're really all one, but we appear
as separate jewels on one net.

Some try to regard everyone and everything
in all they do. Some do less, regard less,
regardless. Some nothing.

THE DIFFERENCE BETWEEN

THE DIFFERENCE BETWEEN NARRATIVE AND DIFFERENTIATION

The Difference Between Residence and Where We Live

"You can tell what's informing a society
by what the tallest building is."
—Joseph Campbell

From the top windowless floor of the Arco
Tower at Flower and Fifth in downtown LA,
my friend and I spit pale white seeds into
the wind and watched them disappear into
the backdrop of the city.

We had risen early, cut high school
for the day, drove the 5 Freeway northbound
out of the clean streets of Orange County.

Tall towers were going up—replacing
the black masonry and gold terra cotta
Richfield Building, built just fifty years
prior from the "Black Gold" riches
of the oil industry. That had nearly tripled
the 150-foot height limit of its time.
These would rise 700 feet, and my friend
and I were going to try to get that high.

So we drove in, parked far away, walked
past homeless day sleepers and shouting
street vendors right up to the site, shadowed
by I-beams, pretended we were adults,
gestured at plywood piles as if we were
working and supposed to be there, lifted tarp
doors and, unimpeded, took the cranky
open-air elevator all the way to the top floor.

No one in the city above us now.
We had made it.

(This, the same thought the white banker
in a high-backed leather chair would think
from that very spot—once the immigrant
workers had finished putting in the windows,
insulating room after room they would never
return to.)

We stepped to the edge and arched our backs
to look up at the giant crane that swayed
and squealed in the winds above us.
Everything ached at such heights, even
our nervous laughs, caught in our throats
from the vertigo of open sky, just daring us
to climb into it.

Sweating and shivering at the same time,
we stared out, pointed wordless at the novelty
of seeing birds from above, their slow
banking on the currents beneath us
leading our eyes northward to gaze
at the fault-bounded block of crystalline rocks
that formed the odd east-west transversing
San Gabriel range—named after the mission,
that was named after an angel, who was called
both archangel and saint by those colonizers
who always shut their eyes as they looked up.

But not us that day.

That mission was once the tallest structure here.
A century-and-a-half later it was City Hall,
which was now a deco dwarf in this
City of the Angels—which itself sits

not on solid rock but shakes
on accumulated sediments
washed from the slopes
of those very mountains—
which are eroding, eroding,
but still tall enough to trap
the moist breezes from the ocean—
the baseline for all elevations,
sparkling at a level below even those saints
on the street—

that man in rumpled linen
interpreting visions all night,
the one my friend and I had asked directions
from when we parked there in front of his
street-level tent, the one whose back was bent
from looking down for so long, who held his
forearm horizontal, then pressed his fist
into his opposite biceps and raised
his other forearm perpendicular,
at a right angle, saying:

"The road goes this way,
but the buildings go the other.
With the riches.
More and more,
every day.
People forget."—

we thought he was going to ask us for money
then, but instead he laughed and pointed,
revealing the way to the highest place,
then reached into the treasury
of his crackling bag
and offered us an orange.

The Difference Between Attendance
and Education

This box canyon behind the campus is
thick with life, insects on the grass and
brush, stacked on branches and aligned
on stalks—like the letters on the pages
of the books in the boxes in the college
dorm rooms, waiting to be unpacked,
spines to the sky. Just like the students
themselves, asleep still, volumes ready
to weigh the shelves. But for now, only
the test of the new mattresses, exhausted
already on the eve of their first day of
classes. Come the end of fall the buzzing
quiets. The canyon still clicks and chirps,
but softer and sparser into winter break.
Spring will bring a new kind of listening.
The theater of nature is never dark. Each
solstice and equinox a threshold that is
crossed, felt or not. This, the first lesson:
To show up every day. To be present.
Next, to cross over from mere existence
and become participants. To measure
the mild degrees of change in light
hour by hour, the slow graduation
of morning colors from midnight
to daybreak. To hear the hillside
roll call then. To be awake for
the quaking of the wildflowers
announcing their presence.

The Difference Between Forgetting Your Wallet and Being Bad at Math

> "If you ask your mother for one fried egg for
> breakfast and she gives you two fried eggs
> and you eat both of them, who is better in
> arithmetic, you or your mother?"

—from "Arithmetic" by Carl Sandburg

Park, grab the shopping list. Mental checklist before opening door: phone, wallet... uh oh. Remember I forgot to take it out of my bag at home. Remember ziploc baggie of coins under the seat. Three baggies, actually. From when I'd emptied the bowl I toss my coins into at the end of the day. Plenty there. Okay. Good to go. Heavy though—so I put the three baggies into one of the larger canvas shopping bags and walk in. Will be embarrassed to count coins. "Why?" I ask myself, "Because you don't want people to think you're poor? How about all that public penny counting in college?" My mind wanders back to those days of bad budgeting and the aftermath of bad choices. Too many to count.

So no, it's not shame over being poor, or people thinking I am—it's holding up a line of people who were smart enough to remember their wallets and are equipped to check out quickly. But I can get what I want. Will count coins fast. Yes. No crowds. Nice. So I shop. Pick an empty lane. Small talk over small change with the cashier as I pluck quarters four at a time from the stash and he fills my canvas bags with the new goods.

With each coin I touch I can smell more of the metallic sharpness that my fingers are yellowing toward. "Imagine how many hands each quarter here has touched..." I say, casually. "If I added them up... How many lives am I connected to with this order?" And then I think of each item in my cart and the many hands involved in the production of each separate ingredient from across the globe, each body who touched each part of each item in my cart, each one with their own money concerns and their own mistakes. Bananas from Columbia. Popcorn from Iowa with sea salt from India. Box designed in Chicago printed with ink made in Mexico.

(Quick math calculation done on way to car afterward: if each coin is ten years old on average, and each touched a new person once per day— wow... hundreds of thousands of people at least.)

"So, I heard that 90% of US bills have traces of cocaine. Do that many people use?" I ask the checker. "Well, clean bills probably get contaminated in bill counting machines," he answers. "And cash drawers." I nod without looking up, still counting my/soon-to-be-his/soon-to-be-the-till's/soon to be the bank's quarters. "Yes, but people who use quarters to buy cauliflower aren't the ones buying the cocaine," I say. The clerk laughs. I lose count. I move my eyes methodically from stack to stack re-counting, and he says: "I heard that every time you inhale, you're breathing atoms that everyone whose ever been alive once breathed."

I exhale and shake my head without looking up. "I don't think that's true." Seven dollars shy. I sigh and resume plucking coins from the bag. "But we're all connected in ways we don't realize, that's for sure," I offer, absently. I then think of adding that people get excited about meteorites and wanting to touch something that once was in outer space yet they don't realize that everything here—including every atom whirring within them—was literally cooked up in the stars, but I was tired and counting the last two dollars to reach the total due and it would take too long to explain and he was now counting himself, sweeping my stacks off the counter and into his open hand and dropping them into to cash drawer tray.

"Here's a penny back." he said. "Thousands of new connections," I said. It didn't connect. "Counting myself." I added. "Okay," he said. "They say if you have change in your pocket at the end of the day, then you're richer than 95% of all people on the planet," I said. "Have a nice day," he said.

The Difference Between Selected and Chosen

The bag of tortilla chips is often picked—
easy to lift in and out, placed there to claim
the parked cart as in use. "Don't take this.
Someone is shopping here!" is the message to
anyone who's looking. Of course, the danger
of selecting such a light item is that it is
just as easy for the opportunist stranger
to pluck out, that jerk who might want to steal
the cart regardless. We've all had it happen,
shocked when we return to the empty place
our goods once were, what we had carefully
selected to be our food, and assumed. We feel
violated. Good mornings can quickly spoil.
Supermarket scruples in action every day.
Idleness in the aisles has a price. This isn't
some mild annoyance. It's a real waste of
time to have a thief walk away with your
cart (even if it squeaked or had a sticky wheel—
perhaps even worse since that had been
the best choice you could find, even if that
noisiness later helps you to locate the twit
who took it, though no way to prove it.)
All that effort in selecting the freshest lime,
the undented can, the latest "use by" date,
wasted. We'll see if there's any cosmic justice
when we reach that final checkout line.

Meanwhile, one wonders if there are similar
rules at play in the Find-a-Mate-at-the-Market
shopping game. It starts with a roll of the dice:
a nosy pass made stealthily from behind
with a glance into the cart of the one that

has caused a spark from afar, who, based
on a glimpse, has been picked as the one
Player One thinks he or she might like to
partner with in a bonus round. Then
comes the assumptions and a card is played,
determined by the ingredients of the meal
they guess is being harvested: onion,
salsa, sour cream, ground beef, oregano—
so they head to the endcap where
the tortillas are stacked and practice
opening lines: "Taco Tuesday?"
or "Do you fry rolled or folded?"
or "Have you ever tried frozen...?"

THE DIFFERENCE BETWEEN DIFFERENTIATION AND WORD PLAY

Our Eyes are Devoured by This World

What if that image burned on our retinas,
an egg, let's say, is really the egg
trying to find itself in us, and we
(being as self-centered as we are)
assume wrongly: sight instead of search.
And the sunlight flung is a star's
groping we sense as heat.

Just as the air hears the star as luminosity,
the starlight embraces the egg
just to sense the hang of its shadow,
just as the darkness enters each lung
of the bear to taste itself hibernating—
each thing's defined by every other thing:
consciousness sparks at every seam of entity.

That smell we smell—the pines, the rich mud
earth after the skies pour—is nothing more
than our own experience, then, of being
tasted by the needles and wet soil; the tang
of the unripe berry wrapped in a gray song
of frost, nothing more than the screaming
feud of acid and ice against our tongue;

and our first whiff of smoke is when the tree—
having changed from bark to flame
to heat to wing of effluvium—comes
to experience the strong
bite of olfactory in order to
taste the thing it once was,
through us, again, at last.

Satellite View

One wilderness connects
to an opening, which connects
to a road, a city, the world.
The borders prove arbitrary
and invented. Just as the wildness
we fight inside us often reveals
not our different-ness (or
differences), but the shared
edges—because the way we
live our lives (for others,
despite) betrays the solitude
(we still feel so often, despite).
Our common acts convey
only unity. Separateness
vanishes when we zoom out
to reveal the whole of it. When
viewed from this perspective,
any focus on "other" is lost.
Elevations and variations melt
like lovers beyond distinction
(as maps tossed into a fire),
and we blur as we soften.

The Difference Between Clearing and Allowance

If we could see a time lapse of the past,
it would be the four-legged ones forging
the paths though the wild first. The two-legged
migrators blazed based on that, no doubt. Jump
cut a million days (to save time) and we
see the paths are now highways (evolving
from trails to roads to boulevards along
the way) with homes and parks and buildings built
alongside and between those arteries.
A constant flow of people, with those there
the latest complaining of the influx,
feeling entitled to call for no more,
how it was better before all the change.

Turning Smaller

Look. See the pinpoint stars
        fade into the glowing dome of dawn:
        can you name the exact breath
        when they surrender into the pale blue
        ocean of morning?

That man, standing, staring as if out to sea—
        could it be he sees something more,
        as the cat at our feet sees the paler
        pinhole suns linger in what we thought
        a starless dawn?

What if we were to know
the moment it all turns—
        clocks,
        pages,
        attitudes,
        heavens?

What if we were aware
of a clicking over
instead of an easing into?
        What if frontiers were clear?
        As the earth shrugs
        away from the sun.
        As the cream turns
        suddenly thick
        in its curdling.
        As doorknobs and dials grow thinner
        with motion, gain friction
        and resistance in stillness.

What if our turning away
from each other were magnified?
If every gesture we stumbled through
amplified—

        we could see then, literally,
        how our stillness shrinks us,
        know that everything grows
        with motion.

Look. See the slow but steady growth
        of the travelers, giants lumbering
        through long life's forests as if ancient
        mammoths across continents.

And there! Tiny monks sitting between
        towering green spears of sequoia
        grass. Or smaller still, silent specks
        of the lotus seed dying under a fallen
        leaf.

And in between, us, in flux:
        speeding together, nearly exploding,
        then just as suddenly stopping unsure
        to wither; then spinning more growth,
        turn and run apart, swelling; slowing
        to turn smaller; stop, shrink,
        and wrinkle.

Slow

If instead of aging we grew slower, imagine
the stillness of such long life, baby faces
preserved as if enhanced, the activity of youth,
lifetimes lived between breaths and blinks.

Imagine the speed of babies in the womb,
somersault flip-flop and sloshing out
into the world with such a rush
the slow sit in slack-jawed awe

of the rapidity of their past.
Once they were that fast.
And though indiscernible at first,
imagine the slowing then at last:

we'd notice our grandparents
in ourselves, see it when we catch
our breath at a glimpse in the mirror,
or slow down long enough to gaze

at the light on the water,
each breath a slowing,
slower still, so
slow

we forget
the platitudes of our decreasing,
memories all of faster selves,
a one-way decay,

deceleration to stasis,
no way to pick up
speed save by
backward glances.

Wrong Number
(The only question worth asking)

Trying to plan my week,
I drew a grid on the page
to slip over the future,
fill in the numbers,
and address the days
one at a
time.

But counting
by days of the week
the spaces between,
I discovered
an extra line drawn,
and so, one too many
days.

I decided to keep it in.
After all, it was due
to arrive tomorrow,
so I might as well wait
and live through it
at least once before
scratching it out of existence.

That being decided, I was faced
next with the question
of what I should do with it.
What could I do?
Save a life?
Buy beans and beer?
Bread and wine?

Or sleep through it,
exhausted from
the previous seven,
then awaken
and begin anew,
maybe even
another eight days?

Let the others remain limited
in their Gregorian litany,
I was growing to like the idea
of this newfound time, whatever
it was called—not having been labeled
like all the other days, no need
to invent a new name now.

The next morning
I was awakened by
my own voice: I had
not heard the phone ringing,
but my pre-recorded
greeting answered
for me.

After the beep,
a person I didn't recognize
began talking about someone
else I didn't know. Being
that this was the first new
day, I thought they might
know something I didn't.

I decided to not pick up,
but to listen carefully
and take their advice
without question, flooded

with relief just to think
that a stranger could know
better about my life than I did.

I'd been wrong too many times,
it was clear. The voice told me
I should forget about yesterday's
mistake, to call that other person
I didn't know and to let them know.
I unplugged the clock
and dialed my birthday.

In the Videotape Rewinding

His hands jerk up at the wrist
as if electrically jolted,

then float calmly down
to rest again

on keys of black
and white.

Fog settles for one beat,
then up again in spasm

between dashes of snow.
Again and again

his stiff torso
awkwardly rocks

as if nerve damaged,
and the song is

gulped back
from the night—

as when perhaps the germ of it
had first filled his lungs,

when the thicker air swam
past his head

and he moved through its cloud
in forward motion

his mouth open like a seine
to gather it in,

to remember the taste,
unfiltered and raw,

ingesting the air willingly,
discovering what had to be said

only by the saying.
Much as we had discovered

hours earlier,
before I sat down

on the empty bed,
before I put the old tape in,

searching
for a part

I'd never seen before,
searching,

remembering
your open mouth,

the sky entering
with its backward logic:

. . . Goodbye.
I love you.

and us together
traveling,

making up,
arguing,

the first touch of your skin,
closeness,

sparks,
your eyes

the first time,
hello . . .

The Last Gesture, Like Their First Dance

The old woman hangs the cup on the hook.
A step. A slip. Her gown flits and billows.

Check how it swings there,
how the creak sounds

within thin walls
holding crushed bone.

The breaks
of that old timeless song.

She closes her eyes, dances backward, a rush
of blood and her dreams swing back with her.

Currents carry all
the basket could gather,

the black river urges it on—
and back—

to when she smelled the fresh perfume
of wood, the spin of the hook's screw,

the twisting wrist
to guide her hand.

Then their first dance and
the whirling brass surging,

remembered after all that time.
The forgotten step found,

yet a slipping
instead of a slide toward.

The slick floor.
A migration song sung in the fall.

How it swings
off the beat,

like the Big Band horns
punctuating

        the dance floor
           bumps.

The warm breath
out

like a current.
The jump.

The hand reaching
out.

      The whoosh!
        The thump.

Breaking Face

(Bathing at the Shore)

I

What if the wave curled in accordance with
all that we forgot? So that the act of falling
was not due to remembering the world
of the newly found face alone (as all other
worlds of sand and glass and shore
and faceless lovers turned suddenly stone
disappeared as remembrance fell,
that we might recall the soft bottom mud
and the thrum of song from deep within,
slow rising like a swell).

II

Try to be less obscure.
What is it you are hiding?
Yesterday you washed your face
and could not remember what it was
she looked like. Today you stared at the wave
as if it held your secret name, a flash upon
the sparkling wall, the past about to shatter
and boom in white madness at your feet,
cool rush of bubbles around your ankles.

III

So what if it did?
What if your sorrow could cling to the rag
and so be washed away? What if the one
you were meant to meet walked past

just as you dropped your grimace
into your cupped hands, rocking and afraid,
and so you missed her? Or what if the other,
who would make your life a song of misery,
turned the corner to see the sharp searching
of your eyes as you looked up, and so
chose to change steps and follow you
into that shade far away from the crowd?

IV

What if there is one holding out her hands
now, as if to offer new sight
as you press your palms
long and hard against your eyes?

The Difference Between Morphology
and Coalescence

Was your waist shaped by my
arm, a river, as you unfolded
from still waters at dawn—
or did you engulf my silent form,
bending me to your wilderness?

Did your hand drape over my
shoulder, a mountain, as you told me
of the ocean daughter's soft song—
or did this lonely mass rise only to form
a place for you to rest?

Will the best of us stay with our balmy
creations, new fountains the gold of
nether flesh, bound only to the earth—
or will a wealth of ceaseless grace yet born
shape anew my hands, your breast?

To the Other Self

I asked the wiser one I would become—
how long have you been seeking me, waving,
patiently calling to tell me to change,
to step onto a better road? How long
have you been shouting, as if underwater,
muffled into the deaf ear of this younger one
cursing at a minor load? I asked myself,
squinting ahead, if I'd keep shouting then,
still reaching through shadows for the one
behind.

I asked another who had come and gone
if she could still recall my voice, or if
a void descends between, a strange curtain
separating my cries from what made me
cry, separating me from wherever it was she
had gone, and I realized that silence
meant nothing certain, heard or not, for her
memory was mine, held out like a bleached
bone divining underground springs for one
ahead.

THE DIFFERENCE BETWEEN
WORD PLAY
AND DIALECTICS

Forgotten Points

I'd agreed
that not
all was what
it seemed—

spider's knees
red dots
small things lost
mite, seed

The Difference Between Assonance and Camouflage

Applause to the one in ten
who can spell "camouflage" correctly
(at least the first time).

"Concealment" (or a stratagem
for it, the way poets bury internal rhymes)
might be easier:

just write "disguise"
or some synonym
when in a hurry and move on.

Choose a word
you're more sure of.
Why sabotage your credibility?

Because who would know
you dodged a word in the first place?
All they see is what you show.

The Difference Between Human and Abstractions

Belief is not an abstract.
It is not the opening of the eyes after a long,
blue sleep—

which is surrender
(which is, in fact, an abstract).
Belief occurs after, when the body rises.

Surrender,
come to think of it,
is not an abstract either.

It is not the throwing up of one's arms
in submission
(another abstract).

No.
It is the decision to allow
the touch of another.

And submission is not an abstract, really—
not the kneeling before the loved one,
as some believe.

It is, instead, the act of opening one's mouth
without indifference (more on this later) to
allow in the breath, name, mouth of another.

Indifference—
not ennui,
but pulling out, away.

To review:
Belief
is the getting out of bed each morning.

Surrender—
offering
of the open hand.

Submission—
the opening of the mouth
for another.

Indifference—
a non-human
act.

What Then is Seen

Between what we hope and what becomes,
an ocean.

Between what we intend and what is heard,
a sky.

If a grid of consequence could be placed
—somehow, laid over—

the chaos of our random acts,
what then?

We might draw a map of our misintentions.
We might see what's not learned from neglect.

Between the imagined plans
and the grasses that rise,

long breaths
that turn to longer sighs.

Between the dream of home
and the place we reside,

a river that turns
and turns.

If a circle encompassing all we have changed
were overlaid beyond our lives

—how A caused B and B begat C—
we might see there is no end to it.

A greater web become apparent.
But what then?

We might weave a story of change,
and thereby change ourselves.

What becomes an ocean: our hope.
What is heard: a sky intended.

How Children Dream vs. How They Sing

Mostly, animals
take the lead roles.

No exact lines.

No exact lines.

Gurgle and whisper,
the filling of lungs,
then a gush into
full-throated joy.

Bizarreness
never appears
as such.

Rolled tongue inhaling.
Surges of nonsense.

Head rocking tick-tock.
A chorus of two words.

Playtime
vignettes
re-emerge.

Melody swoops
like a butterfly's
tracings.

Often
there's hunger.
Not often fear.

Tiny legs
hugging a bough,
bare feet dangling.
A blue mist
smudging

No complex narrative.
No exact lines.

A white cloud floats
in the heart of the lake
like the one above.

The Difference Between Form and Definition

profile of wings
against night air
      vs.
           contour of warm breath
           displacing sky

shape my name takes
in the darkness of your mouth

     vs.

        form of swimmer
        defined
           by tides

grace of gesture
      across black

        vs.

                ease of ego upon holy

    loss of all
in mind that imagines
      shape of god

           vs.

       God

how birds sing vs. how they fly

I swore I'd always love you
but now can't remember your face

aqueous humor of the eye
retains the ancient sea

the bird of death sings notes that weep
with bits of song held in the breeze

I'd lied
broken words flown

blinking
back

tweep
chirp and glide

Between Ellipses

.

. .

Tell me
what consumes you
is important, then think of

the first law of thermodynamics,
the conservation of all, even the mundane:

how the gray hair of the grandmother gets torn
from soft scalp, tangled in loops and knots, wound
around bristles—not lost but one—as both get tossed
into a clear plastic bag, put into a larger bag, dragged
out to the curb under the palm in Long Beach, then lifted
and tipped into a cacophony of rotting rinds and rags, hauled
with cans and keys and cranky glass in a groaning truck, driven
away and dumped onto a layered hill of similar obscurity (to be). . .

begins to melt and meld under a different law now—how the dark
purple nozzle of the broken hair dryer slides easily into the slick
open mouth of a can of creamed corn, the wrapper of which
tickles the face of the smiling boy in the photograph
behind cracked glass, and as that boy will age
and forget, the pigment will likewise fade
until the greasy rat that makes its home
in the shade of the burnt orange lace

of an iron pot's graceful decay
eats a pale scrap of smile,

cheek: squeezed to scat
pellet, shat to melt
back to black

. .

.

The Difference Between Atlas and Axis

Hills sweep up and away defying trapezoidal routes along the long warm valley left in shade. Beneath the soil bones lie broken. For how long has it been like this? The vertebral song of decay.

The coffee brews to help awaken. Birds flap and trill to assist in finally looking up. Most days go by with both above and below unnoticed: hard up, soft down, feather, wing and whistle. Black dot of nostril and yellow bill: the smallest things lost. The dull ache with movement. The bruise hung heavy and blue beneath the skin, like night. No sin. No sign.

The hills sweep away. You sweep up. The ridged valley falls to shade. It is late. To exist within a birthblue seam changes the face unnoticeably each day. Bruises surface, fade. A song erupts from what the swallows bring. Eyes weep from swallowing such largeness. At the sound of the breath gasping—there! In the ground the depth of three bird beaks: two breasts and one wing, uncovered while looking for something else. As if to say: Awaken. As if to say: Stop grasping. The hard song of your suffering can be released. So sing. So sing.

THE DIFFERENCE BETWEEN DIALECTICS AND SCIENCE

Abandonment is to Impermanence
as Displacement is to...

In the old house,
smooth tide pools of erosion on a dial
where thumb and index have pinched
and twisted, seeking only change.

    (The hobo nails his foot
      to the freight car floor.)

Mammalian oils coagulate
in the grooves of a key.
Dull knobs are polished to mirrored moons
with countless arrivals and departures.

    (The pull of the earth's molten core
      drives buried bones deeper.)

A paper cup is drained and crumpled.
Cracked wax. Mosaic walls. Stained windows.
Wrinkles on a faded photograph.
The iron kettle corrodes to orange lace
in the sunlight of the junkyard.

    (The skywriter laps back and forth
      over the tattoo parlor,
      spelling "FOREVER"
      one thin cloud string at a time.)

Half

(Interhemispheric asymmetry of the
  electro-encephalographic sleep patterns
  in dolphins and other mammals that
  may or may not mate for life)

A sphere halved
sits flat as two domes
and neither rolls.

(The ocean surface heaves, veined white
  and cold like slabs of marble, but far
  below the Black Sea Porpoise sleeps
  in a tunnel of calm—each half
  of the brain taking turns to sleep:
  just one hemisphere alert, and one or
  the other eye open at all times.)

We said we shared one mind
then parted.

(The Glaucus-winged Gull
  flip-flops the same in
  half-brained sleep,
  but only for one-fifth
  of the night.)

I cannot sleep at all.

Apertures

The lost cat finds
a dark patch of pooled rain,
still and black, and smells
her thirst quenched in
the mud-scented night.
But a perfect circle,
glowing near the edge,
she mistakes for a full bowl of milk,
and what she had sought for so long
suddenly is not what she wants,
and does not satisfy—
the dish shatters into ripples,
her head a quick blur
matching the moon,
the quaking at such plain treasure.

> There are holes
> glowing at the top
> of the sky.

The same moonlight
will be sliced
into
glowing beams
of ghost bamboo
by gaps between leaves,
high and still
above a forest floor—
but no one
is walking
there now.
The two who wandered

earlier will not
be fooled by such
arrogant deception.

            There are holes,
            small and certain,
            in the roof.

The couple tumbles
as one,
unaware
that the footprints
they left without thought
are now filling with silver—
sunken foundations for
a staggered row of trees
to come.
Afterward, once their
breathing unconsciously
slows and syncopates,
a thumb will slide lightly
across, like the moon—
a small, cloudy drop.

The Difference Between Mountain and No Mountain

I had not realized
that what is neglected
manifests elsewhere: a phrase of movement,
the grace of an athlete slowed by first
a twinge, then an ache, soon
a hobbling universe.
      (the discarded glove
        retains the shape
        of the missing hand)

What is carried,
nagging, translates into gestures:
unconscious tics and glances,
changing the flow, reshaping the motion
that otherwise would have been,
the way a rock redirects the current.
      (the marrow hum
        of ancestors shapes
        the hang of skin)

A formation unknown.
What goes unnoticed congeals
into rocks, then boulders. Larger.
So much to amend. Only now
do I see: not active reshaping,
but conscious breathing.

      (moving stones
        at the back
        of my mind)

Earth sans Moon
(vs. embraces from the stranger)

Without our moon as muse
this rock would flip-flop,
chaotically wobbling, its axis
drawing zeroes across the darkness.

      (but she floats there,
        and you are pulled,
          ravished by the strange one who flatters
        in some ancient tongue—the long-
        voweled name of the lost child)

Without our moon, no eclipses.
No lunar calendars. No word "month"
rising from a word meaning "moon"—
because, no moon.

      (the architect, enamored by her moan—
        the rumble of a shifting deep within,
        stone against stone
        as the buried fault settles—allows
        the burning beam to collapse into ashes)

No dancing under the full disc of cream.
No lunacy. Simply an ink black sky,
but brighter stars.
Brighter stars.

      (the strange bird sings
        the colors of his throat,
        engulfed
        in the gray
        ocean of dusk)

The earth spins much faster, this way.
Tides of lag, not gravity.
And shorter days.
And shorter nights.

> (the silhouette twirls
> atop the ridge,
> unnoticed until dawn,
> arms still held wide
> to hold the night)

Stronger winds too:
the planet banded
like Jupiter
from the friction of sky.

> (aching to lose herself into more,
> the dancer leaps—
> the creek whispers
> its way downhill,
> toward relief)

The moderate seasons are gone now.
Eons of fire,
followed by winter.
Then no change at all.

> (love: the dream
> of fever
> from one
> who sleeps
> in snow)

Forgive Me

There were four plums sitting
on the counter, arranged in an arc:
section of circle defying the angle
of light slanting cadmium blue
through the dusty pane.

We'd yet come to see
the ritual of dismount:
shift of sun and tone
from each of our arrogant perches.
Breakfast, you took one, left three.

Down to two by afternoon's emergence:
opposite poles only straight-line logic
could come between—
and forgetting what was said in haste,
I realized they were nectarines.

ACKNOWLEDGMENTS

The author wishes to thank Pattiann Rogers for her poem, "The Importance of the Whale in the Field of Iris," which inspired the first "The Difference Between" poem decades ago, and eventually this entire series.

Also, heartfelt thanks to the editors of the following publications for being the first to bring the following poems to a wider audience:

"Headlong, Unforgiving" was first published in *Poetry/LA*, Spring/Summer, 1989.

"Forgive Me" was first published in *Poetry Digest*, Fall, 1996.

"The Difference Between Repair and Reconstruction" was first published in *WTC Remembrances*, September, 2002. It was later anthologized in *Poets Against the War*, February, 2003.

"The Difference Between Salt Water and Blood" was first published in *Re)verb*, Fall 2003.

"The Difference Between One and Reunion" was first published in *Zócalo Public Square*, April, 2013.

"Between Ellipses" won the Kick Prize for Poetry, 2013.

"The Difference Between Rattle and Settling" was awarded the 2014 Nancy Dew Taylor Award for Excellence in Poetry, and was first published in *Emrys Journal*, 2014.

"The Difference Between Restraint and Gravity" was first published in *Blue Fifth Review*, Summer, 2015 (Sand).

"The Difference Between The Thread of the Current and the Present" and "The Difference Between Entropy and Evaporation" were first published in *Anastamos*, 2017 (Fluidity).

ABOUT THE AUTHOR

Grant Hier is the Poet Laureate of Anaheim, California. He was the 2014 recipient of Prize Americana for his book *Untended Garden*, which was published by The Poetry Press in 2015, and nominated for both an American Book Award and the Kate Tufts Discovery Award. He was awarded the Nancy Dew Taylor Prize for Literary Excellence in Poetry in 2014 for his poem "The Difference Between Rattle and Settling," and the Kick Prize for poetry in 2013 for his poem, "Between Ellipses." Several of his pieces have been nominated for a Pushcart Prize. His poetry has been anthologized in *Orange County: A Literary Field Guide* (Heyday, 2017), *Only Light Can Do That* (Rattling Wall/PEN Cener USA, 2016), and *Monster Verse—Human and Inhuman Poems* (Knopf/Everyman, 2015).

Individual poems have been widely published internationally, including in *Emrys Journal, Dallas Review, Poetry Digest, Poets Against the War, Zócalo Public Square, Review Americana, Blue Fifth Review Quarterly, WTC Remembrances, Pearl, Poetry/LA, Chiron Review, Orange County Review, Orange Coast Review, RipRap, Re)verb, Slipstream, City Dialogues, Tandava, Faith, Stymie, Word Riot*, and others. Three fiction pieces were included in *LA Fiction Anthology: Southland Stories by Southland Writers* (Red Hen Press, 2016). His fiction, reviews, and essays have been widely published as well, including in *The Review of Contemporary Fiction, Jeffers Studies,* and *Explorations in English Studies*—as well as in the books *Teaching Composition with Literature* and *John Fante: A Critical Gathering.*

He has served as editor, managing editor, and editor-in-chief of several literary journals and magazines. In addition to writing, he is a musical artist, visual artist, graphic designer, and former art director. He recorded his original musical compositions for A&M Records in Los Angeles, and his installation art has been featured in several gallery showings. As a voice actor, he contributed the part of Stanley Hohner for the Audio Book version of the New York Times Bestseller, *Lincoln in the Bardo: A Novel* (Penguin / Random House, 2017) by George Saunders.

Grant Hier earned his BA in English at California State University at Fullerton, and both an MA in Literature and MFA in Creative Writing Poetry at California State University at Long Beach. For more than a decade he served as Chair of Liberal Arts and Art History and Faculty Senate President at Laguna College of Art + Design where he remains as Full Professor, teaching courses in literature and creative writing.

More at www.granthier.com

CPSIA information can be obtained
at www.ICGtesting.com
Printed in the USA
FSHW01n2232010518
47685FS